To _____

From _____

Published by Lion Children's Books
an imprint of
Lion Hudson plc
Wilkinson House, Jordan Hill Road,
Oxford OX2 8DR, England
www.lionhudson.com/lionchildrens

ISBN 978 0 7459 6271 9 (Blue edition)
ISBN 978 0 7459 6272 6 (Pink edition)
ISBN 978 0 7459 6038 8 (Gift edition)

First edition 2006

Blue edition 2011
Pink edition 2011
Gift edition 2011

A catalogue record for this book is
available from the British Library

Printed and bound in China,
May 2016, LH06

BABY'S Little BIBLE

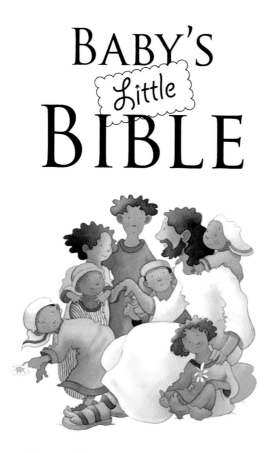

Retold by Sarah Toulmin
Illustrations by Kristina Stephenson

LION
CHILDREN'S

Contents

Old Testament

New Testament

Old Testament Stories

The Old Testament stories
are about the God who made
everything in the world.

In the beginning

Once upon a time there was nothing.

God spoke: 'I want light.'

Wow!

The world began.

Then God made everything
in it.

Wow!

God was pleased.

God made man. 'Your name
is Adam,' said God.

God made woman. 'Your name
is Eve,' he said.

'Take care of this wonderful world,'
said God.

Rainy days

One day, God looked down from heaven.

'Oh dear,' said God.

'The people have spoiled my wonderful world.'

Then God remembered Noah. Noah was a good man.

'I have a plan,' said God to Noah.
'I'm going to start the world again.
I need you to build a big boat.'

Noah obeyed.

'Take your family on the boat,'
said God.

'Take two of every kind of animal.'

God sent the rain. It rained and rained.

Splish!

Splash!

Splosh!

The boat began to float.

It floated up
high.

It floated
back down.

20

BUMP!

The water trickled away.

'Come out of the boat,' said God. 'Start the world again.

'Look at the rainbow!
It shows my promise:
I will keep the new
world safe for ever.'

God chooses a family

Once there was a
man and his wife.
They were sad.

'We don't have children. We won't have grandchildren.'

The wife looked at mothers and children, and she cried.

On a starry night, the man heard
someone speaking.

It was God.

'Listen, Abraham,' said God. 'You
and your wife Sarah will have a child.
You will name him "Isaac".

'He will have children. His children
will have children.

'Your family will grow and grow.

'They will be my people. I will look after them.'

Abraham and Sarah loved their little baby Isaac.

A special coat

Isaac had a son named Jacob. Jacob had lots of children. He liked Joseph best.

Jacob gave Joseph a very special coat.

'I'm special,'
boasted Joseph.

Joseph's big brothers were cross. 'We don't want you,' they said to Joseph.

'Go away and stay there!'

They asked some men to take
him away.

They went to Jacob. 'Something bad has happened,' they said.

'Joseph has gone.'

'We found this bit of his coat.'

Jacob sobbed. 'Poor, poor Joseph!' he said.

33

In a faraway land, God looked
after Joseph.

The king of that land put him
in charge of important things.

One day, Joseph's brothers came to the land. They went to the man in charge.

They didn't know it was Joseph, but Joseph knew them.

'We need to buy food,' they said.

'Hmphh,' said Joseph. 'I'm not sure I trust you.'

In the end, Joseph wanted to be friends again.

'I'm your long-lost brother!' he said. 'Come and live in this land.'

'Hooray!' they all said. God had kept them all safe.

A new home

The mother and her little girl were crying.

'We must hide baby,' they agreed. 'The wicked king is hunting boy babies.'

They hid the baby by the river.
A princess found him.

Together, they all agreed to keep
baby Moses safe.

When baby Moses grew up, he
found out how wicked the king was.
He made people work very hard.

One day, God spoke to Moses through a burning bush. 'You must help my people,' said God. 'Take them away from the wicked king.'

Moses went to the king:
'Let the people go,' he said.
'Let them find a new home.'

'No,' said the king.
'No, no, no!'

'I will make the king change his mind,'
said God to Moses. 'I will guide the
people to a new home.'

'You lead the way. I will make
a path through the sea.'

'Hooray!' said the people.

'God is our God. We are God's people.'

They set out to find their new home.

Walls fall down

Moses grew old.

Joshua was brave and strong.

'Please lead the people to their new home,' said Moses.

'Come on,' said Joshua to the people. 'We're nearly there.'

The people came to a great big city with great big walls and great big gates.

'Oh dear,' said Joshua.

'Listen to me,' said God. 'March round the city. March every day.'

Day 1

Day 2

Day 3

Day 4

Day 5

Day 6

Get ready...

Day 7

Ta-dada-da!

'Hooray!'

CRASH!

The city walls fell down!

'God has let us into our new home,' said Joshua. 'God loves us, and we must love God.'

The giant and the boy

The giant's name was Goliath. He was very fierce. He didn't like God's people.

He really scared them.

'Ha! ha! ha!' laughed Goliath. 'Come and fight me!'

The boy's name was David.
'I'll fight you,' he said.

'Ha! ha! ha!' said Goliath.
'You're very small.'

'Ha! ha! ha!' said Goliath.
'I've got a big sword. You've
only got a handful
of stones.'

'I trust in God,' said David.

He slung a stone.

THUD!

Goliath fell to the ground.

David was only small, but he put his trust in a great big God.

The big fish

God spoke to Jonah.

'Please go to Nineveh. The people there do bad things. Tell them to stop.'

Jonah sulked. 'I don't like the people in Nineveh. I don't want to go there.

'I'll go
   somewhere else.'

He came to the sea.

'Where is the boat going?'
asked Jonah.

'Spain,' said the sailor.

'I want to go there,' said Jonah.

'Come aboard,' said the sailor.

That night, God sent a storm.
The boat rocked.

'Help!' shouted the sailors.

'Oh dear,' sobbed Jonah.
'It's all my fault. I disobeyed God.'

'We do feel sorry for you,'
said the sailors. 'But...'

SPLISH!

Jonah sank into the deep,
deep sea.

A big fish came by.

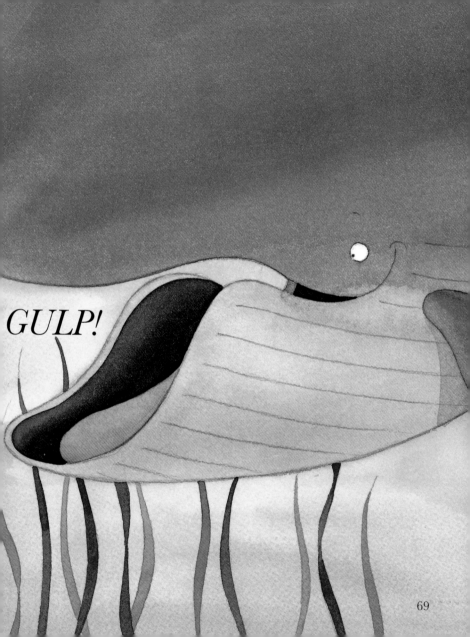

GULP!

Hiccup!

'Oh,' said Jonah. 'God kept me alive.

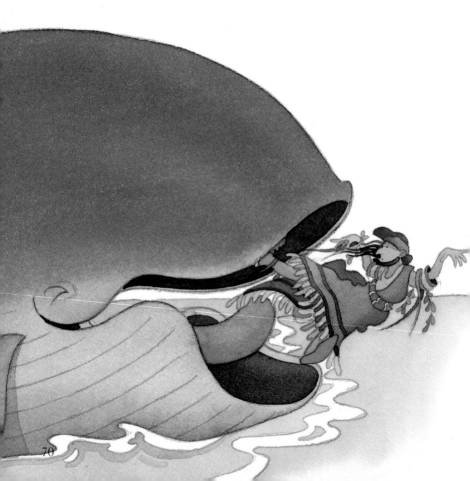

'What shall I do? I know! I'll go to
Nineveh. I'll tell the people to stop
doing bad things.'

The people of Nineveh listened
to Jonah.

'Oh dear!' they said. 'We have
been bad.'

'Sorry, God,' they cried.
'Please forgive us.'

And God did.

73

Hungry lions

Daniel loved God. He talked to God every day.

'Help me to do what is good and right,' he prayed.

Daniel also worked for the king.

'He's my best worker,' said the king.
'I'm going to give him the best job.'

The other workers were cross.

'Let's get Daniel into trouble.'

'Let's tell the king to punish people who say prayers.'

'Then we'll tell him about Daniel.'

'Hee hee hee.'

The plan worked.

'Sorry, Daniel,' said the king. 'I've been tricked.'

Daniel had to go into the pit of lions.

'God bless you,' said the king sadly.

'*GRRRR*,' said the lions
hungrily.

But God kept Daniel safe.

'Hooray!' said the king.

'Daniel is still my best worker.

'And Daniel's God is the best
in the world.'

New Testament Stories

The New Testament stories
are all about Jesus.

Baby Jesus

One day, God sent an angel with a message.

'Hello Mary,' said the angel. 'God has chosen you. You are going to be a mother. Your baby will be God's son. You will call him "Jesus".'

Mary was puzzled.
She was also a little
bit afraid.

Joseph was puzzled too. 'Mary is the one I want to marry,' he said. 'What shall I do now?'

Then an angel came with a message.

'Please marry Mary. Please look
after her.'

'I will,' said Joseph. 'We
will be a family.'

Together they went to Bethlehem.
They had to stay in a stable.

Mary's baby was born there.

She didn't have a cradle. She laid
Jesus in a manger.

Out on the hillside were shepherds.

Then an angel came with
a message.

'God's son has been born
in Bethlehem.'

'God is going to bless
everyone on earth.'

More angels appeared.
They sang happy
songs.

91

The shepherds went to Bethlehem. They found baby Jesus.

'The angel was right,' they said to each other.

'Your baby must be very special,' they said to Mary.

High in the sky, a bright star shone.

Far away, some wise men saw it.

'God has put the star in the sky
to tell us a new king has been born.

'We will go and find him.'

They went to Bethlehem.

They brought gifts:

gold,

 frankincense

 and myrrh.

They were gifts for a king.
They were gifts for God's son.

Jesus and his message

Baby Jesus grew up.

He was a good son.
He worked to help his family.

He was also God's son. He had work
to do for God.

'Listen,' he said to the people. 'I have good news.

'God loves you. You are God's children.

'Look at the birds: God takes care of them.

'Look at the flowers. God takes care of them.

'God will take care of you.'

It was a lot of work to tell the good news.

Jesus chose friends to help him.

Some were fishermen. Jesus saw them by Lake Galilee. They were in their boats. They were catching fish.

'Come and follow me,' he said.

They left everything to be
with Jesus.

Then he chose more friends.
They all left their jobs.

'We all want to follow Jesus,' they agreed. 'We all want to help people love God.'

Jesus had many other friends.
They helped too.

'We all want to be part of God's
family,' they said.

The hole in the roof

The man lay on his bed.
He looked at his friends.

'Where are you taking
me?' he asked.

'We are carrying you to Jesus.'

'You can't walk.'

'Jesus can make people better.'

Then they saw the crowds.

'We can't get through the door,'
said the friends.

'Hold tight. We're going up to the
roof. We can make a hole in it.'

In the house, the
people heard noises.

tap

    tap

tap

    scritch   *scratch*

       scritch   *scratch*

'Look out, Jesus!' shouted someone.
'Something big is coming.'

It was the man on his bed.

Jesus smiled. 'God forgives you,' he said to the man.

'Now get up and walk.'

'What's all this!' said the crowd. 'What do you mean, Jesus?'

'He means I can walk!' laughed the man. He picked up his bed and walked away happily.

The good shepherd

Jesus told a story.

'A shepherd had a hundred sheep.

One went missing.'

'The other sheep will be safe here,' said the shepherd.

'I must go and find my lost sheep.'

He set off.

plod

plod

plod

At last he found it.

He carried it home.

He put it safely to bed.

He had a party to celebrate.

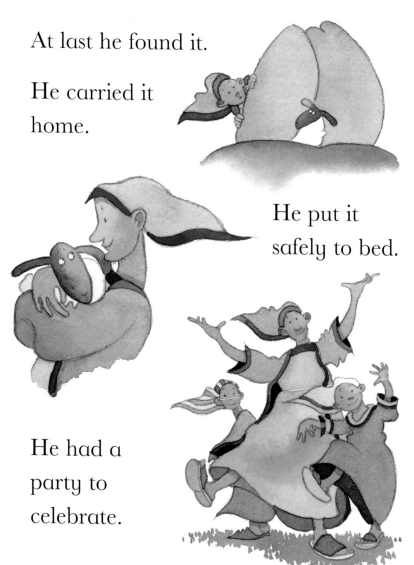

'God is like the shepherd,' said Jesus.

'God's children are like the sheep.

'When a little child comes to God,
God is very happy.

'Up in heaven, all the angels sing.'

Bread and fish

Lots of people came
to listen to Jesus.
They sat and
listened for
hours and
hours.

'I'm hungry,' said a little girl to her mother.

'Oh dear,' said her mother, 'so am I! We forgot to eat.'

Everyone was very hungry.

'Jesus,' whispered his twelve friends. 'The people need to go and buy food.'

'We can feed them,' said Jesus.

'How?' asked the friends. 'Only this little boy has any food.'

'I've got five loaves of bread and two fish,' said the boy. 'Jesus can have them.'

Jesus took the bread
and fishes.

He said a prayer.
'Dear God,
Thank you for
this food.'

He gave some to each of his twelve friends. 'Please share this with the people,' he said.

By a miracle, there was food
for everyone.

'Enjoy the food,' said Jesus.

And they did.

A scary storm

One day, Jesus and his twelve friends were on a boat. They wanted to go across the lake.

Jesus was tired. He fell asleep.

Suddenly, the wind blew. The waves crashed.

'Help! Help! Help!' cried the friends. 'Wake up, Jesus! The boat is going down!'

Jesus stood up.

He spoke to the wind: 'Hush.'

He spoke to the waves: 'Lie still.'

They obeyed at once.

'Why were you afraid?' said Jesus.

The friends did not know what to say.

'Jesus is an amazing friend,' they agreed.

The little girl

Jairus was very worried.

He rushed to see Jesus. 'My little girl is very poorly. Please come and make her well.'

Jesus went. All kinds of people seemed to get in the way.

At Jairus' house, everyone was crying.

'The little girl is dead,' they wailed.

Jesus went to her bedside.

'Little girl, get up,' he said.

At once, the little girl sat up.

Her mum and dad clapped and laughed.

Jesus had made them happy again.

A prayer

Jesus talked to God every day.

Sometimes he sat in his room to say his prayers.

Sometimes he walked over the hills.

'Teach us to pray,' said his friends.

Jesus told them a short prayer.

Our Father in heaven,

Your name is amazing.

We want everyone to see that you are king.

We want to do the things that make you happy.

Please give us the things we need.

Forgive us when we do wrong.

Help us forgive others.

Keep us safe, now and always.

Amen.

Here comes the king

One day, Jesus came to the big city called Jerusalem.

He was riding a donkey.

The people saw him.

'Here comes the king!

'Here comes the king!' they cried.

They waved palm branches.

Jesus and his friends had a meal together.

They shared bread together.

They shared a cup of wine.

'Remember me when I am gone,' said Jesus.

The cross

Not everyone liked Jesus. They sent soldiers to take him away.

The soldiers nailed him to a cross.

And there Jesus died.

Jesus' friends were very sad.

At the end of the day, friends came to take Jesus' body. They put it in a tomb.

They used a big round stone as a door.

'Goodbye, Jesus,' they said. 'It's all over now.'

They went home sobbing.

Night came.

Alive!

As soon as they could, some friends went back to Jesus' tomb.

The door was open.

The tomb was empty.

Angels spoke: 'Jesus isn't here.

'He's alive again.'

Then the friends saw Jesus.
'God can put everything right,'
said Jesus.

'Go and tell everyone in the world.'

So they did.

Blessing

Little one, rest your tired head

May angels watch over you in
your bed.

May God's love surround you
through the night

And keep you safe till morning light.

Amen.